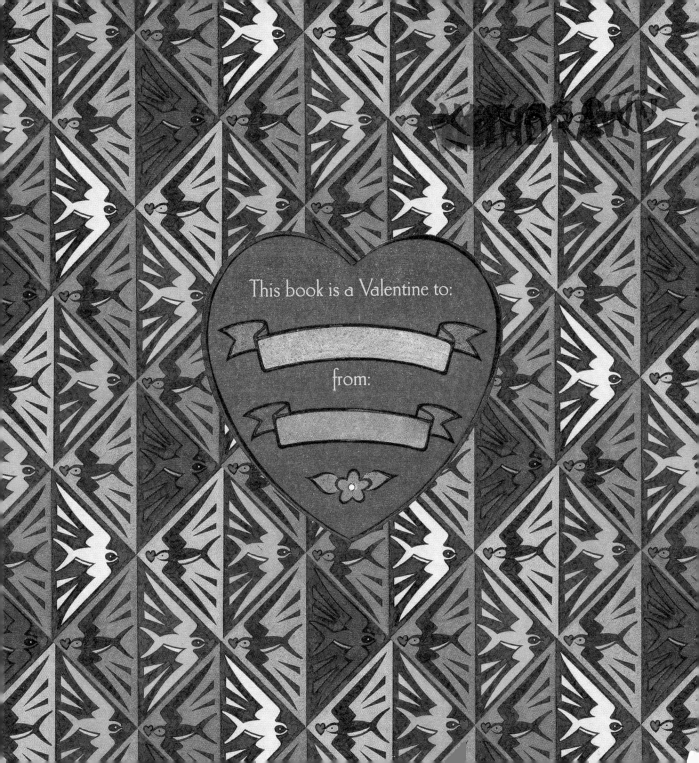

This book is a Valentine to:

from:

The Story of
VALENTINE'S DAY

by Clyde Robert Bulla
illustrated by Susan Estelle Kwas

NEWLY ILLUSTRATED EDITION

HarperCollins*Publishers*

The text for this book was first published in *St. Valentine's Day*, a Crowell Holiday Book edited by Susan Bartlett Weber, written by Clyde Robert Bulla and illustrated by Valenti Angelo in 1965. Text copyright 1965 by Clyde Robert Bulla. Copyright renewed 1988 by Clyde Robert Bulla.

The Story of Valentine's Day

Text copyright © 1965 by Clyde Robert Bulla. Text copyright renewed 1988 by Clyde Robert Bulla. Illustrations copyright © 1999 by Susan Estelle Kwas

Library of Congress Cataloging-in-Publication Data

Bulla, Clyde Robert.

The story of Valentine's Day / by Clyde Robert Bulla ; illustrated by Susan Estelle Kwas. — Newly illustrated ed.

p.   cm.

"The text for this book was first published in St. Valentine's Day, a Crowell Holiday Book . . . in 1965"—T.p. verso.

Summary: Relates the history and describes the customs of this holiday from its beginning in Roman times to the present. Includes directions for making a paper valentine and sugar cookies.

ISBN 0-06-027883-8. — ISBN 0-06-027884-6 (lib. bdg.)

ISBN 0-06-443626-8 (pbk.)

1. Valentine's Day—Juvenile literature.   [1. Valentine's Day.   2. Holidays.]

I. Kwas, Susan Estelle, ill.   II. Title.

GT4925.B83   1999

394.2618—dc21

97-37195

CIP

AC

Typography by Elynn Cohen

Visit us on the World Wide Web!

http://www.harperchildrens.com

❖

ed and pink hearts, flowers and chocolates, cupids and doves, cards and letters with sweet or silly sayings written on them—all these things mean it's Valentine's Day!

Valentine's Day is celebrated each year on February 14. It is a day to give small gifts of love and friendship to someone special. These gifts are called valentines. But how did February 14 come to be a day to think about love?

No one knows for sure. Valentine's Day is one of our oldest and most mysterious holidays.

More than two thousand years ago, a holiday similar to Valentine's Day was celebrated in Rome. But in those times the Romans did not call it Valentine's Day. They called the holiday Lupercalia. Lupercalia means "feasts of Lupercus."

The early Romans believed that a god named Lupercus protected them from wolves and looked after their crops and animals. They honored Lupercus by singing and dancing and feasting. Lupercalia came later in the Roman calendar than our Valentine's Day does, so Lupercalia was also a festival to celebrate the beginning of spring.

On the night before Lupercalia, girls would write their names on pieces of paper and place them in an urn. Boys would take turns drawing names. The girl whose name they chose would be their partner for all the games and dances. Often the pair would become engaged at the end of the festivities. This romantic custom reminds us a bit of Valentine's Day today.

For hundreds of years, the Romans celebrated Lupercalia. But after the Christian religion came to Rome, many Romans no longer believed in such gods as Lupercus. Still, people loved celebrating Lupercalia and did not want to give it up. So the Church decided to use the holiday to honor a priest. They renamed the holiday "St. Valentine's Day" and celebrated it on February 14.

Legend has it that this holiday was named after a Christian priest who lived in Rome almost two thousand years ago.

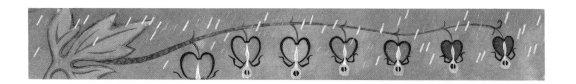

Church records show that there were actually several priests named Valentine living back then. According to one story, Valentine was arrested because he refused to pray to the Roman gods. In prison, Valentine became friends with the prison guard and his blind daughter. Finally, after many years, the priest was called before the Roman emperor Claudius II, or Claudius the Cruel. Claudius told the priest he would be set free if he gave up his religion. Valentine refused—and even tried to convince Claudius to become a Christian!

Claudius flew into a rage and ordered the priest beheaded. But before he was taken away, Valentine asked the prison guard to give a note to his blind daughter. As soon as the girl opened the note, her sight was miraculously restored and she was able to read what was written on the piece of paper: "From your Valentine."

Another story tells how a priest named Valentine disobeyed a Roman law in the name of love. Claudius the Cruel had forbidden young couples to marry because he needed a fierce army and believed that single men made better soldiers. Valentine broke the law and married young couples in secret.

When Claudius found out, he was so angry he had Valentine killed. And so St. Valentine's Day was a celebration of courage and friendship in honor of a brave priest, but it was also a day to think about love and romance.

Celebrations of Valentine's Day spread to other countries. During the Middle Ages, people in England believed that birds returned from the south to choose their mates around February 14. So Valentine's Day seemed like a perfect time to choose a sweetheart.

Many of the English celebrations were like those of the Romans. People feasted, played games, and danced. But the English began to add a few of their own customs.

In one, a girl would write boys' names on pieces of paper, roll each paper into a ball of clay, and drop them into a bucket of water. When the clay balls fell apart, the first paper to surface would reveal the name of the man the girl would marry.

It was also during the Middle Ages that Valentine's Day became a children's holiday. English children went from door to door in groups singing songs. The mistress of the house would often throw flowers or pennies to the children or give them sweet buns made with plum filling. Here is one of the songs the children sang:

"Good morning to you, Valentine.
Curl your locks as I do mine—
Two before and three behind.
Good morning to you, Valentine."

In Italy, young men and women gathered together in flower gardens on Valentine's Day to listen to music and poetry. In France, fancy dress balls were popular. Young Frenchmen were often expected to present their Valentine's Day dance partners with bouquets of flowers.

When young couples in Austria, Hungary, and Germany first celebrated Valentine's Day, they also danced and went to parties. But later, the holiday became a more serious one. It became the custom for boys in these countries to draw the names of saints instead of the names of girls on February 14. For a whole year, the boys were expected to live like the saint whose name they had chosen.

The very first valentine was written at this time, about four hundred years ago, by a French nobleman named the Duke of Orleans. He was taken captive during a war and imprisoned in a tower in England. He missed his wife very much, and wrote her many love letters. Many of the letters mentioned St. Valentine. One of them reads:

Wilt thou be mine? Dear love, reply,
Sweetly consent, or else deny;
Whisper softly, none shall know,
Wilt thou be mine, love? Ay or no?

As more and more people learned how to read and write, they decided to send this kind of letter to their sweethearts. Soon the letters came to be called valentines. They were often decorated with hearts, flowers, birds, and cupids. In Greek and Roman myths, Cupid was a mischievous god who flew around shooting people with his invisible arrows. These arrows made people fall hopelessly in love.

By the early 1800s, many people were decorating their valentines with satin ribbons and lace. For people who needed help thinking of what to write, there were little booklets they could use called "valentine writers." Inside there were poems for the old and young and for every occupation, such as soldier or baker.

Valentine's Day was particularly popular in England while Queen Victoria ruled the land. Paper valentines made during this time are called Victorian valentines. They were usually delicate and rather fancy. Today, people collect Victorian valentines. Many of them can even be seen in British museums.

Although people also gave each other flowers and candies and jewelry at this time, Victorian valentines became a favorite way of expressing feelings of love. In England, February 14 became the post office's busiest day of the year.

Early American settlers did not celebrate Valentine's Day. The first pioneers were too busy struggling to survive. Valentine's Day didn't catch on in America until the mid eighteenth century.

Many of the first American valentines were proposals of marriage. The popular "True-Love Knot" and the "Endless-Love Knot" were mazes drawn in the shape of connecting hearts that had messages of love written inside the pathways.

In the "pinprick" style, sewing needles were used to create fancy borders by poking holes along the edges of the paper. Another popular valentine during this time was the "acrostic," in which the first letter of each handwritten verse spelled out a sweetheart's name. Handmade cards were popular in America until the mid nineteenth century.

Valentine's Day is still observed in many countries, but it is most popular in the United States and Great Britain. In England, children still receive candy and money, and men and women still send cards and flowers to their sweethearts.

In the United States, people young and old give each other cards, flowers, candies, and jewelry. Bakeries are filled with heart-shaped cookies and cakes. There are still Valentine's Day dances, and it is believed to be one of the most popular wedding days of the year.

Children also celebrate Valentine's Day in the classroom with parties and games. They make their own valentines with construction paper and glue. They decorate boxes with crepe paper, doilies, and cutout hearts so that friends can place the valentines inside. Perhaps decorating boxes for homemade valentines is a modern version of the old Roman custom of drawing names from an urn or a bowl.

Many things have changed since Roman times, but for hundreds of years, February 14 has been a day to honor love and to cherish those who are close to us. It is also a day to think about how old customs and beliefs can mix together and blend into something new.

OLD-FASHIONED "PINPRICK" VALENTINE

You will need:
1 piece of construction paper (standard 8½ x 11)
Sharp pencil or ballpoint pen
Colored pencils or crayons

1. Fold the piece of construction paper in half.
2. On one side of the folded paper, lightly draw a picture of a heart with a pen or pencil. Be creative! Make a border around the heart. Add anything you like!
3. Carefully make "pinpricks" along your drawing with the point of the pencil or pen. The "pinpricks" should be as close as possible without touching.
4. Once you have finished "pinpricking" your entire drawing, fold the construction paper back over.
5. Write a special valentine message on the inside of your card with colored pencils or crayons.

Tim

Together forever,
In good or bad weather,
My funny valentine.

Lisa

Let me say,
in this nice way,
St. Valentine's is fun,
and you're my special one!

Will

Will you be my valentine?
I'll be yours & you'll be mine,
Let's be friends & let's not part.
Love is what comes from the

VALENTINE COOKIES

1 cup (2 sticks) butter, softened
¾ cup sugar
1 egg
2 tablespoons milk
⅛ teaspoon lemon extract or
   almond extract (optional)

½ teaspoon vanilla extract
3 cups flour
1 teaspoon baking powder
½ teaspoon salt
Red sugar sprinkles, red-hot
   candies, or colored frosting

Lightly grease a cookie sheet. In a large bowl, cream the butter and sugar until smooth. Add the egg, milk, (optional) extract, and vanilla extract. Beat well. Mix flour, baking powder, and salt together in a small bowl and then add to batter, stirring well.

Divide the dough into three parts and flatten each into a disk. Wrap each disk in plastic wrap and refrigerate for 30 minutes. Preheat oven to 350°F. Roll each disk out on a floured surface to 1/8" thickness. Cut the dough with heart-shaped cookie cutters and place hearts on cookie sheet.

Bake approximately 8–12 minutes or until lightly browned around the edges. Cool on wire racks. To decorate before baking, dust with red sugar sprinkles or red-hot candies. After cookies cool, they can also be decorated with colored cake frosting.